CONTENTS

THE GARDEN
OF THE
LORD

THE GARDEN
OF THE
LORD

WALKING WITH GOD IN THE QUIET PLACE OF YOUR HEART

WENDY ROBBINS

WinePressPublishing
Great Books, Defined.

WinePress Publishing (PO Box 428, Enumclaw, WA 98022) functions only as book publisher. As such, the ultimate design, content, editorial accuracy, and views expressed or implied in this work are those of the author.

ISBN 13: 978-1-4141-2239-7
ISBN 10: 1-4141-2239-X
Library of Congress Catalog Card Number: 2012910115

Dedicated to the Lord

ACKNOWLEDGMENTS

Special thanks to:

My gifted illustrator, Jane Boeckman; Paul Boeckman, for his technical assistance; Lynn Sonia and Judy Wagner, for their editing in the initial stages of the book; and the many people who gave me prayer support and encouragement in the writing of this book.

INTRODUCTION

In the place where He was crucified there was a garden.
—John 19:41

GOD'S WAYS ARE not always our ways. When we choose to follow the Lord, our walk can lead us down some very unusual paths. Several years ago, the Lord spoke to me about "forsaking all" and following Him to the mission field. I was a single parent with two teenagers. I lived in a beautiful suburban home, had a good job as the accountant for the church I attended, and also led a ministry to women in a correctional facility. While on a ten-day mission trip, the Lord touched my heart in a powerful way, giving me a strong desire to pursue missions on a long-term basis. There were many issues to deal with in order to do this, but everything began to fall into place as He prepared my family to leave what was secure and familiar and set out for the unknown.

In the fall of 1990, we left Minnesota for a missionary training base in Wisconsin and subsequently, foreign outreach. At the time, I felt this would result in long-term missionary work on foreign soil. I home-schooled the children while I was taking classes, and the three of us were also trained to participate in an outreach team. The focus of this program was missions, and also development of our personal relationship with God. We also learned about the importance of maintaining a balanced family life.

One day, towards the end of the training phase, the Lord quietly spoke to me. I felt a strong impression in my mind that at the end of the outreach (after five months), I was to return to Minneapolis with the children. At first I thought, *What kind of contradiction is that? You sent me here, Lord … You had me sell our home, leave my job and ministry, family, and friends!* In spite of my protests, I sensed the Holy Spirit saying in my heart, *The relationship between your children and their father is more important at this time in their lives than a missions calling upon your life. They need the nurturing he gives them—they need both parents.* Even though their father had given full approval for me to take them to the mission field on a long-term basis, my heavenly Father had something else in mind.

I felt pierced through my heart. A vision died inside me that day and tears streamed down my face. At the same time, I sensed God very close to me. I felt directed to read the story of the crucifixion. What could the death of Jesus possibly have to do with this situation in my life? It seemed odd. I picked up my Bible and started reading a passage in John 19. When I came to verse 41, the words practically leapt off the page. "Now in the place where He was crucified there was a garden." The Lord was showing me that this was the death of a vision for me—I must lay it all down, *but* it would be a place of new growth in my walk with Him—like a *garden* experience. It didn't matter that it seemed contrary or that it looked odd to others; what mattered was that it was His will for us to return home, just as it was His will for us to go. Even missions can't be more important than obeying His voice. I was reminded of the verse, "To obey is better than sacrifice" (1 Sam. 15:22). I thought I was making a "sacrifice" by being willing to go on the mission field, but obeying His voice was more important than my sacrifice. I gave up my rights that day and laid down the missionary call at His altar with much grief.

That is when God put me on another path ... A journey that He opened up to me to find out what this "garden" experience means. It has been both a wonderful and often a difficult walk of discovery that brought about this book.

The end of one call of God was really the beginning of another—the beginning of something new in my heart and life.

CHAPTER 1

THE JOURNEY TO THE GARDEN

A PLACE OF THE HEART

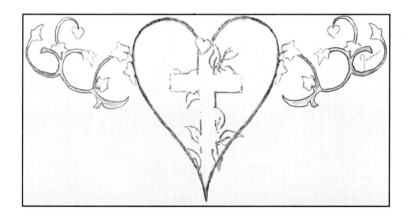

A garden enclosed is my sister, my bride.
—Song of Sol. 4:12

THE JOURNEY INTO the garden of the Lord began as the Lord opened up the Scriptures to me, revealing many verses and passages referencing the word "garden." There are various gardens represented in the Bible: the garden of Eden, the garden

1

of Love in the Song of Solomon, the garden of Gethsemane, the garden of Betrayal, the garden of Crucifixion, and the garden of Resurrection. These were places, but what happened in them? And what do they mean to us in our Christian walk?

Our Heart as the Garden

The Lord began showing me that there was more significance to this word "garden" than merely being a place of growth. Through more study, much writing, and revelation from the Holy Spirit, He unfolded the concept of thinking of my own heart as a garden (His garden). The Greek word for heart, *kardia*, is used figuratively in the Bible for the "hidden springs" of our personal life, the center of man's inward life. It includes the emotions, reasoning, and will.[1]

This is a garden belonging to the Lord where He is to find His joy—a garden which is to be for His pleasure. It is symbolic of our life with God, or in other terms, our "heart relationship" with Him. Song of Solomon speaks of this garden in verse 4:12 (KJV). "A garden enclosed is my sister, my bride; a spring shut up, a fountain sealed." The believer is pictured as a watered garden set apart for the Lord to bring forth fruit for His delight.

What is A Garden?

The Hebrew word for garden is *ganna*, a place hedged around, an enclosed area protected by a wall or hedge.[2] It comes from the same root word, *ganana*, as is used of the protective guardianship of God, like a mother eagle (see Isaiah 31:5). Webster defines a garden as "an enclosure; a plot of ground where plants are cultivated; a rich, well-cultivated area protected by a wall."[3]

The necessary elements for a garden are soil, seeds or plants, water, sunshine, and fertilizer. We can make spiritual analogies from each of these elements to our own lives as Christians.

SOIL is the foundation for healthy seed and plant growth. Soil resources are critical to the plant's development, as plants are dependent on the organic matter in the soil for nutrients and energy. Soil provides minerals and water to plants, and as it absorbs rainwater, it prevents wilting of the plant. Soil is the habitat for many living organisms. Plants living above ground have spent part of their life cycle below ground. There is a tight connection between above-ground and below-ground life cycles, making good soil of utmost importance for healthy plant growth in a garden.

Good soil in our hearts is the foundation for healthy spiritual growth. In the parable of the sower, the "good soil" is the man who hears the Word of God and understands it, and as a result, bears fruit (see Matt. 13:23). The Word of God gives nourishment to our souls and is the life-giving instruction book for us. As we absorb the Word of God, like rainwater, it is absorbed into the soil of our lives, preventing drought and wilting. It is rich and goes deep within, providing the resources critical to an environment in our heart where the seed of God's Word will flourish.

SEEDS are meant to reproduce themselves and continue to bring forth life. In order to produce a plant, a seed is planted in the ground. It appears lifeless and is hidden from sight. The apostle Paul, in 1 Corinthians 15:36, speaks of this seed when he says, "Every time you plant seed, you sow something that does not come to life ... unless it dies first" (TAB). Jesus was referred to as the "seed of the woman" in Genesis 3:16 where the promise of redemption was first given. The death and resurrection of the individual seed of Jesus Christ gave us life.

The word "seed" is used in other figurative ways in the Scriptures, referring to the "word of the kingdom of heaven," "the children of the kingdom of heaven," "the word of God," and the "kingdom of heaven" itself. Our hearts are meant to be fertile ground where God can plant good seeds to reproduce His life in us.

3

WATER, next to air, is the most essential element to our survival. Water makes up more than two thirds of the weight of the human body, and without it, we would die in a few days. Water is mentioned in the Bible more often than any other material resource and is used symbolically for salvation (see Isa. 12:3): "With joy you will draw water from the wells of salvation." John 2:5 says, "Except a man be born of water and the Spirit, he cannot enter the kingdom of God" (KJV). Ephesians 5:26 speaks of Christ sanctifying the church by the washing of water with the word." John 7:38-39 speaks of the Holy Spirit: "He who believes in Me ... 'from his innermost being shall flow rivers of living water.' But this He spoke of the Spirit."

The symbolic elements of water are essential to our spiritual survival and growth. Water is a blessing. When the earth drinks, things grow. As the garden soil absorbs the gentle rains, the root system reaches down, going deeper for more nutrition. As the roots go deeper, the plant pushes through the ground and grows stronger and taller.

Jesus said He would pour out the Holy Spirit upon those who would come to Him and drink. To drink is to receive from Him, and as we do, His Holy Spirit becomes a well of living water within us to quench our thirst and flow out as a river of life to bless the lives of those around us.[4] I visualize this as a well so deep, filled with water that will never run dry even though we keep drinking from it as we go deeper with the Lord. I see the way we are nourished with the water of the Word, and how necessary this water is for us to become all He wants us to be. I see the refreshing, living waters of the Holy Spirit who is living inside of us, flowing in and through us like a beautiful fountain of life.

SUNLIGHT fuels all life on Earth. Plants use the energy of sunlight in a process known as photosynthesis which creates a pathway to growth.[5] Jesus Christ is our "light" and God has created a pathway to Himself through His Son so that we might receive spiritual life and grow in Him. The very first recorded words of God are "Let there be light" (Gen. 1:3). It is significant that God, Who is light (see 1 John 1:5), began His creative design of the world with light. The word "light" is also used metaphorically in Scripture in many places. In the Old Testament, it is used as an image of prosperity (see Job 22:28), of life itself (see Ps. 56:13), of instruction (see Isa. 2:5), of the guidance of God (see Ps. 119:105), and as a powerful contrast to darkness (see Ps. 112:4). In the New Testament, light is symbolic of the nature of God (see 1 John 1:5), of the glory of God's dwelling place (see 1 Tim. 6:16), and of Jesus Christ (see John 1:4; 8:12) who stepped into the darkness as the "Light of the World."

FERTILIZER produces faster growth and healthier, longer-lasting plants. There are different types of fertilizers. Seeds and new growth need a *fast-acting fertilizer* to get them off to a good start and to get the strongest root system in place. Time-release fertilizers are best used after plants have started growing because the slow release provides a constant rate of food over a longer period of time. The best fertilizer is compost made up of dead organic plant material that is mixed with fresh green materials. Everything needs time to cure or rot. There are wonderful advantages to a natural compost pile in gardening. Nutrient-rich material is produced by the decomposition and causes better water retention and better drainage to the garden.

When we first become Christians, there seem to be many outward things that we "die" to right away as we hear the Word of God and experience the conviction of the Holy Spirit, especially if we are coming out of a lifestyle that is clearly opposite to the Lord's plan. Then we experience a new growth spurt. Over time, we need to add more "dead" material to the compost pile of our hearts along with new, fresh nutrients the Lord feeds us in order to keep growing. The advantage of allowing the Lord to compost the dead material in our lives is that the decomposition of that dead stuff will then produce nutrient-rich soil to help us grow up in Christ in a healthy, life-giving way as the water of the Holy Spirit is poured into us, absorbed, and allowed to flow out of the healthy soil of our hearts.

CHARACTERISTICS OF BIBLICAL GARDENS

BIBLICAL GARDENS WERE ENCLOSED

Biblical gardens were enclosed by a wall or hedge. The garden of our heart is also to be a protected place—walled off for the Lord as in Songs of Songs 4:12. Satan likes to break down the wall and destroy our holy separation to the Lord. It is important for us not to leave ourselves open to the enemy. When we do, we become like a garden trodden down and trampled underfoot. The enemy gets in when we do not keep on the path of separation to the Lord. Satan may bring in his enticements, but we need to be alert to them and make responsible choices not to follow him. If we do not guard our hearts, something as innocent as our own longings can lead us down a wrong path. Then circumstances may arise that tempt us to compromise our own convictions. In my own life, the enemy attempted to break down my own holy separation to the Lord by trying to tear down two things I hold very dear in my walk with the Lord: integrity and purity.

After coming back from the mission field, I was hired by a company as an accountant. I discovered in a very short time that I would be required to report false financial information, and I was also a witness to some other very unethical business practices. I needed to terminate my employment, but there was a problem. I had purchased a home and I was to close on it in a few weeks. How could I be unemployed? Was I going to choose integrity and trust God, or was I going to choose dishonesty and compromise? I chose to leave the company after working there for only three weeks. God, in His faithfulness, secured another job for me on the very same day that I closed on my home! He will always honor our faithfulness to Him.

In a separate work situation, I was faced with dealing with inappropriate behavior from a boss. Purity was something very important in my life and I was shocked at this type of behavior. I had to confront him, and as a result, endured humiliation as he found many ways to degrade me. God provided a way out of the situation when a new job opportunity opened up, giving me a much better future with additional pay.

It is often difficult to stay in that protected place with the Lord when faced with uncertainty and temptations, but it is definitely worth it! God always has a better way for us! He places boundaries around us for good reason. When we stay in that protected place with Him, we actually experience more freedom.

BIBLICAL GARDENS WERE IRRIGATED BY WATER

In addition to being enclosed, the gardens in biblical times were irrigated by water. Again, in Song of Songs 4:12, the believer is pictured as a "spring sealed up" or a fountain sealed. In the east, pure water springs were often found in gardens and they were so precious to their owners that they were walled about and locked to keep them free from pollution and impurities.

Jesus gives us "living water" as He fills us with the Holy Spirit. He tells the woman at the well in John 4:14 that, "Whoever drinks of the water that I shall give him shall never thirst; but the water that I shall give him shall become in him a well of water springing up to eternal life." This water flowing through us is a pure fountain of water in our hearts that needs protecting from pollution and impurities. We are so precious to the Lord that He wants us to be kept free from anything that might pollute us. The pure water also results in much abundance in the garden. "I the LORD am its keeper, I water it every moment, lest anyone damage it, I guard it night and day" (Isaiah 27:3). The Lord is very interested in guarding and protecting His garden—our heart.

BIBLICAL GARDENS WERE A REFUGE FROM THE HEAT

Gardens in biblical times were shaded places where one could come to get relief from the heat. The Psalms are filled with verses about God as our refuge. Psalm 121:5-8 says, "The LORD watches over you—the LORD is your shade at your right hand; the sun will not harm you by day, nor the moon by night. The LORD will keep you from all harm—He will watch over your life; the LORD will watch over your coming and going both now and forevermore" (NIV). When the "heat" of stresses, trials, temptations, and just doing "life" comes, the Lord welcomes us to come into that place of refuge with Him. This is where we get refreshed!

BIBLICAL GARDENS PRODUCED FRUIT, SPICES, HERBS, VEGETABLES, AND GRAPES

They were provision for food, medicine, preservation, and healing. Biblical gardens were places that provided for the whole person. What was produced there had many purposes, and the Lord has many purposes for the fruit He produces in our lives. Our fruit comes from the Lord and not from our own self-efforts. Hosea 14:8 says, "From Me comes your fruit." Ezekiel 47:12 speaks prophetically of a river where "leaves will not wither, and their fruit will not fail. They will bear every month because their water flows from the sanctuary, and their fruit will be for food and their leaves for healing." This is a picture of continuous fruit-bearing as we receive "water" directly from the sanctuary of the Lord Himself. As believers, the Lord gives us this fruit of the Holy Spirit so that we may give it out to others.

BIBLICAL GARDENS WERE LOCATED AWAY FROM "CROWDED PLACES"

Gardens are cool places of refreshment and retreat. These are the places we come to be with God. He gives us renewal when we come to that place with Him in the garden. Jesus himself often went away to a quiet place to be alone with the Father, and He instructs us to do the same in Mark 6:31: "Come away by yourselves to a lonely place and rest a while." There is a beautiful book, *Come Away My Beloved*, by Frances J. Roberts that the Lord has used in my life many times. The book is filled with words Frances received from the Lord for all of us—words that speak into specific circumstances in our lives. The book helped me find a quiet place of communion with the Lord, sense His presence, and respond to His guidance. These two quotes from the book speak directly to coming away with Him: "Rest in Me. Wait upon Me. Come apart with Me. Seek My face. Seek My fellowship," and "COME AWAY MY BELOVED, and be as the doe upon the mountains; yes, we shall go down together to the gardens."[6]

This heart relationship with God is a very special, intimate place. It is not meant to be confining, but rather, this is where we receive our very life—the life separated unto Him and belonging to the Lord. This is the "Garden of your Heart."

Chapter 1

Reflections in the Garden ...

1. What three words come to mind when you think of the word "garden," and how can you relate them to your heart?

_____

_____

_____

_____

2. As you reflect upon your heart as a garden belonging to the Lord, are there parts of you that you have not given to the Lord?

_____

_____

_____

_____

3. What circumstances in your life do you think "crowd out" intimacy with the Lord?

_____

_____

_____

_____

PRAYER

Father God,

Thank you that our hearts are intended to be special places belonging to You. Enable me to be willing to give my whole heart to You. I choose to give You any parts of me that I have held onto (name them). Draw me away from all the crowded places in my life and draw me into intimacy with You. In Jesus' name, amen.

CHAPTER 2

THE GARDEN OF EDEN

A PLACE OF DELIGHT

And the Lord planted a garden toward the east, in Eden.
—Gen. 2:8-10

GOD CREATED A garden where Adam and Eve could walk with Him daily and He provided everything they needed, and where they had an intimate relationship with Him. It was a place for them to enjoy one another and find delight in each other.

The Hebrew meaning for the word Eden is "a place of delight" and that is God's intention in our fellowship with Him. He wants us to experience *mutual delight* in one another. The true meaning of "place of delight" means "to be pleased with, to enjoy, to have favor with, and to see as valuable."[7]

OUR DELIGHT IN THE LORD

We are meant to enjoy the Lord—to value our relationship with Him. When we delight in Him, He plants His desires in our hearts. "Delight yourself in the Lord and He will give you the desires of your heart" (Ps. 37:4).

"You give them to drink from the river of delights, for with You is the fountain of life" (Ps. 36:8-9). Note the word "with" used in this verse, as well as above in the definition of "delight." This became very significant to me when I realized that I had unconsciously thought I was doing various things "for" God—entering into Christian service, missionary work, giving of my money, prayer groups, etc. Instead of doing things "for" God, we are to enter into a partnership "with" Him. We are together with God in whatever He leads us to do.

GOD'S DELIGHT IN US

We often think in terms of what it is about God that gives us delight, and God wants us to experience delight as we reflect on the wonderful aspects of His character, love, faithfulness to us, power, and unchanging nature—all His incredible attributes. But one day He posed this question to me, "What do you think gives Me delight?"

The obvious is that He delights in us just because we are His, and this is very true. But I felt He was urging me to discover some things in the Scriptures that are really pleasing to Him in our life with Him. Here are some truths I learned:

"He delights in unchanging love."

—Micah 7:18

The Hebrew word for love in this verse, *hesed*, means "loyal, steadfast, or faithful love" and stresses the idea of those involved in the love relationship belonging together.[8]

"Let him who boasts, boast of this, that he understands and knows Me, that I am the Lord who exercises loving-kindness, justice and righteousness on earth, for I delight in these things, declares the Lord."

—Jeremiah 9:24

He loves it when we get to know Him better—when we personally come to understand who He is.

"For you do not delight in sacrifice, or else I would give it; You do not delight in burnt offering. The sacrifices of God are a broken spirit, A broken and contrite heart—These, O God, You will not despise."

—Psalm 51:16-17 NKJV

God does not need our outward sacrifices if they are performance-based and are nothing more than empty, religious rituals. He wants us to sacrifice with a sincere heart. He desires a relationship with us where we give out of a heart of love for him—whether it's in worship, service, finances, or anything else we give him.

An example of this in my life is that upon returning home after our brief missionary experience, I thought it would be good to find a "hole in the wall" type of house or apartment to rent for my children and myself and to look for a part-time job so I could still pursue short-term mission trips while raising my children. I thought I was making a real "sacrifice" for God by renting inferior housing. I don't think God was especially pleased with my plan. I found different places I thought would be suitable to rent, but in every case, the door slammed in my face. I was not accepted as a renter even though I had the necessary finances. Someone else would get there first and the place would already be rented by the time I arrived. After three weeks of this, as well as being separated from my children (we were all staying in temporary housing with friends and/or relatives), I realized something must be wrong. Didn't God want us to live together as a family? What was the point of coming back if I couldn't even find a place for us to live? I laid the whole situation before the Lord in prayer and asked Him what was hindering me? A light went on as He spoke to my heart, "You are refusing to put roots down!" Of course, He was exactly right! I did not want to get too established because I wanted to be mobile. However, the Lord didn't ask me to be mobile. He wanted me to establish a secure home for my family and to support my children's relationship with their father. I had missed what would delight God and it really broke me before the Lord.

What He wanted was a broken and contrite spirit. I was now in a position to hear where He wanted us to live. Within days, God worked through my sister and provided a home for me to buy that was located five blocks from her home and in the school district where my children wanted to attend school. It was an incredible blessing as we put down our roots there!

"The steps of a man are established by the Lord; and He delights in his way."

—Psalm 37:23

When we follow the Lord and allow Him to order our steps, He is pleased.

"Behold, My servant, whom I uphold … My chosen one in whom My soul delights."

—Isaiah 42:1

"This is My beloved Son, in whom I am well-pleased."

—Matt. 3:17

Of course, the Father delights in His Son, Jesus and the Father is delighted when we follow in the footsteps of Jesus Christ. Jesus loved spending time with His Father while walking on this earth, and they were and are together in their love relationship.

The Lord established the garden of Eden as a place of delight for Adam and Eve (and symbolically for us) and Himself. He not only gave them (us) the gift of enjoying a relationship with Him, but also made the garden an amazing place! God Himself planted it. It was the epitome of God's perfect creation—a perfect setting. It was pure and clean, and there was lush vegetation and beautiful plants that were pleasing to the eye. It was a well-watered garden with rivers flowing through it. The garden of Eden was fruitful and full of abundant provision. The Bible says in Genesis 1:12 that the earth brought forth vegetation, plants yielding seed and trees bearing fruit with seed in them and that God looked at it and saw that "it was all good." The seeds were meant to reproduce what God had created.

The most significant of everything in the garden of Eden was that God's presence was there. He loved walking in the garden and fellowshipping with His creation. He established a plan that was meant to protect and nurture His relationship with man. He gave man a job to do in the garden. He placed boundaries in the Garden, and He gave man choices.

MAN'S JOB IN THE GARDEN

A description of the job God assigned to man is found in Genesis 2:15. "Then the Lord God took the man and placed him into the Garden of Eden to cultivate it and keep it." Adam was "placed" (Hebrew *nuah* means "set to rest") in the garden to cultivate and work it (Hebrew *abad* means "to serve"). This wasn't a striving kind of service, but rather a restful experience. Rest in the Christian life comes through complete reliance on God's promises and full surrender to His will. (Hebrews 4 talks about this rest, which we enter into through faith.)

Man was to keep, cultivate, and tend the garden and we are to cultivate the garden of our heart. It belongs to God. Therefore, we must take care of it. A garden is best cultivated by tilling, feeding it well with fertilizer, and rooting out the weeds.

Gardeners will tell you that what makes the best fertilizer is a mixture of dirt, dead plant material, and manure—the compost described earlier. We can relate this fertilizer in our lives as a death to self. I struggled very much with this as I laid down the call to long-term missions. It was the death of a vision, something God had planted in my heart, and yet I had to let it die. How do we reconcile this type of death when it happens to us? I sensed this was what God wanted. My life with God had been severely tested. As I left the missions organization, the song, "My Life Is in You, God," kept going around and around in my head. "My life is in you, God; My hope is in you, God; My strength is in you, God...."[9]

I had felt my life was going full speed ahead with vision and direction, then suddenly, it all came to a halt. It was like coming to the edge of a cliff where the road ends and just drops off into nothingness. Have you ever felt like that? I felt as if I was wandering around in the darkness and began to question whether or not my life really was in God.

God wants us in a place where our life truly is "in Him" no matter what the circumstances are. Perhaps you are dealing with health issues, grief, relationship problems, addictions, financial struggles, or a job situation. There is always something in this life that tries to pull us away from our "center" in the Lord. This is why it is so necessary to cultivate our heart relationship with Him and die to self.

A garden is cultivated by tilling the soil to keep it free of weeds. It must be well-watered and kept free of pollutants. We, too, must let God till up the sinful "weeds" in our life garden. We have to let Him stir up our faith as we determine to lead a pure life. In Christ, we are "sanctified, cleansed, washed by the water of the Word" (Eph. 5:26).

BOUNDARIES IN THE GARDEN

God established boundaries in the garden of Eden that were designed to protect Adam and Eve. He told them they could eat from any tree in the garden except the Tree of the Knowledge of Good and Evil. He commanded them not to eat from it and warned them that they would surely die if they did. God wanted the absolute best for man.

Satan, in the form of a serpent, was also in the garden of Eden. Why do you think God allowed him to be there? Some of the reasons could be choice, free will, and testing. There was a boundary drawn and God gave man a choice to stay within the boundary or cross over it. The test was man's choice to obey or not. It was the boundary God set. There are choices to make in the garden of our life and the enemy is going to be hanging around, offering various temptations trying to get us to make the wrong choice and go the wrong way, crossing the boundaries God has set for us.

The two trees in the garden: the Tree of Life and the Tree of the Knowledge of Good and Evil were both found in the middle of the garden, very close to one another. They could very well represent two choices. Maybe the two trees were so close to each other that the choice Adam and Eve made could be rationalized. There is often a fine line between obedience and disobedience. How many times in our own lives have obedience and disobedience seemed so close that we rationalize the compromise and wrong choices we make?

God's plan was for man to eat of the Tree of Life. This tree was meant to preserve and promote life. Satan's plan was experimental, tempting man with experiencing the knowledge of good and evil because he knew that such knowledge would destroy the relationship Adam and Eve had with God. How often are we tempted to experiment and taste of things that God never meant for us to taste or experience?

Satan's questions were designed to suggest that God is not good and fair because He was restricting Adam and Eve from eating the fruit of one of the trees. Adam and Eve fell into the same three categories of temptation that are found in 1 John 2:16:

1. The lust of the flesh,
2. The lust of the eyes, and
3. The boastful pride of life.

Their sin, like ours, was more than just eating forbidden fruit; it was disobeying and rejecting the Word of God, believing the lie of Satan, and placing their own wills above God's will. The consequences of their choice resulted in the fall of man and Adam and Eve being driven out of the garden of Eden. They were now blocked from the Tree of Life and separated from God.

The garden of Eden, "place of delight" was designed by God for intimacy with Him. He provided everything that man could ever need for a fulfilling life. It was His original plan that we would walk in His ways with Him and experience all of the beauty of this garden. His desire was and is for us to choose Him and to value Him the way He values us. When man sinned, the door to the garden experience designed by God was shut, but His heart and His plan was and is to restore our lives to His original intention. The rest of the Bible takes us on a journey that always, always points to restoring our relationship with God. There are more gardens to experience along the way.

Chapter 2

REFLECTIONS IN THE GARDEN ...

1. How does taking delight in the Lord express itself in your life? In what ways do you think God takes delight in you personally?

    _____

    _____

    _____

    _____

2. What things are you "doing" for God? Do you think He has led you into these things as a partnership with Him, or are you doing them out of obligation or a desire to do "good works"?

    _____

    _____

    _____

    _____

3. In what ways can you cultivate the garden of your heart?

    _____

    _____

    _____

    _____

4. Think about boundaries. How do boundaries protect us—emotionally, physically, and spiritually? Are there boundaries in God's Word that you resist?

_____

_____

_____

_____

PRAYER

Father God,

Thank you that Your desire for us is to enjoy a mutual relationship of taking delight in one another. Enable me to see the ways You delight in me and draw me into a life of delighting in You. Thank you for making full provision for everything I need and for placing boundaries of protection in my life. I choose to walk with You and embrace Your boundaries. Help me make right choices in my life—choices that will please You. In Jesus' name, amen.

CHAPTER 3

THE GARDEN ENCLOSED

LOVE WITHIN THE WALL

I am my beloved's and my beloved is mine.
—Song of Sol. 6:3

SOLOMON USES THE metaphor of a garden to represent our love relationship with God. This garden is a protected place and to get to it, we must walk on the path of separation away from the enticements of the world, keeping a wall of holiness

23

around us. This is where we turn away from the world and become solely His. Separation becomes an intimate place, not a confining one, as we become God's hidden one. Gardens in the East were walled off because they needed to be protected. They were precious resources. We, too, are God's precious resource and we are enclosed by Him when we keep our hearts for Him. There is a hedge of protection around this garden and all the powers of darkness cannot penetrate that hedge.

CHARACTERISTICS OF SOLOMON'S GARDEN

IT CONTAINED PURE WATER SPRINGS THAT WERE SEALED OFF TO PROTECT THEM

> "A garden locked is my sister, my bride, A rock garden locked, a spring sealed up."
> —Song of Sol. 4:12

Pure water springs were found in many of the gardens of the East, and as previously mentioned in chapter one, they were carefully locked up and sealed to keep them free from pollution and impurities. Again, this was because water was such a precious commodity. The goal of our hearts, as well, must be to keep ourselves pure because we are so precious to the Lord. This water flowing in and through us is the pure fountain of water in our hearts, giving us the power to lead an unpolluted life which will result in abundant fruit. Song of Songs 4:15 says, "You are a fountain *springing up* in a garden, a well of living waters and flowing streams from Lebanon" (TAB). There is a sense here of the vertical relationship we have with the Lord as He fills us with His water, and the horizontal relationship of using that water to reach out to others.

Jesus gives us the ability to live this way because He is "living water" for us. He fills us with His Holy Spirit. Jesus, speaking to the woman at the well in John 4:14, says, "But whosoever takes a drink of the water that I will give him shall never, no never, be thirsty anymore. But the water that I will give him shall become a *spring of water* welling up (flowing, bubbling) [continually] within him unto (into, for) *eternal life*" (TAB, emphasis mine). In John 7:38, we read, "He who believes in Me—who cleaves to and trusts in and relies on Me—as the Scripture has said, Out from his innermost being springs and rivers of living water shall flow (continuously)" (TAB).

It was planted with fruit trees, herbs, and flowers

"Your shoots are an orchard of pomegranates and a paradise with precious fruits."

—Song of Sol. 4:13 TAB

God plants this garden for His own pleasure. It is a place of beauty filled with blossoms and flowers and fruit. In H. A. Ironside's book, *Addresses on the Song of Songs*, he says, "What precious fruit is found in the heart of one who is shut-up, sealed in the Lord."[10]

The Hebrew word for "plants" is translated as "sprouts" or "shoots." "Orchard" means "paradise," and speaks of the garden of Eden, in which God intended all believers to partake. It is a place where our hearts produce fruit that is for God. It is a paradise and a place where He finds His joy and delight in us.

The plants in a heart that belong to the Lord have certain characteristics:

They are growing: "... God was causing the growth."

—1 Cor. 3:6c

They are of high value: "For you have been bought with a price" (1 Cor. 6:20). What higher cost could there be than the precious blood of Jesus Christ?

They are a sweet fragrance to God and man: "… the sweet aroma of the knowledge of Him in every place."

—2 Cor. 2:14c

They are profitable and of great use to God: "Walk in a manner worthy of the Lord, to please Him in all respects, bearing fruit in every good work and increasing in the knowledge of God."

—Col. 1:10

They are permanent—preserved by God: Even when the flowers wilt above the surface, the roots remain grounded and will once again bear fruit. Watchman Nee, in his book *The Song of Songs,* writes about how it is God's grace that lasts forever and causes us to blossom over and over again for Him.

Solomon lists the types of plants and trees found in the garden. The plants are beautiful in color and fragrance. Some of them give off fragrance as the rain and dew fall on them. This gives us a picture of the Holy Spirit, with the reoccurring theme of the living water of Jesus Christ, filling us and flowing in and through us. Other plants send a subtle aroma when the rays of the sun warm them. This reminds us that as we bask in the light of the Son, we become a sweet aroma. Some plants never give out their fragrance until they are *pierced* and the sap flows. Jesus Christ was pierced for us and His blood was poured out for us. We "share in the sufferings of Christ" (2 Cor. 1:5), and our own suffering and trials often result in a fragrance that would never be released without pain.

The Bible is full of symbolism. Sometimes we have to dig deep to discover the symbolism's meaning and make it relevant for our lives. I was very excited as I made discovery after discovery while studying the plants in Solomon's garden:

1. **Pomegranates** symbolize "abundance of fruit," and are full of edible, sweet seeds. Orchards of pomegranates are said to be some of the most beautiful. They are filled with choice fruit that is rich and nutritious. As we grow to be spiritually mature, we, too, experience fullness and fruitfulness. Some hold the view that the pomegranate may be the fruit of the Tree of Life in the garden of Eden (Gen. 2:9; 3:22). It is also listed in Deuteronomy 8:8 as one of the fruits of the Promised Land. The pomegranate was symbolic of the fruit of the priesthood (Ex. 28:33). A design of pomegranates was woven into the high priest's robe in blue, purple, and scarlet material and speaks of the fruit of righteousness. The pomegranate is also referenced in 1 Kings 7:18–20, where the tops of the pillars of Solomon's temple were carved with 200 pomegranates.

   The plants we bear as a result of our Christian growth are to be as this orchard of pomegranates: life-giving and filled with righteousness. Hebrews 12:11 tells us that the "fruit of righteousness is peace."

2. **Henna** or "camphor" is a small shrub or tree that bears cream-colored flowers which hang in clusters like grapes and are highly scented with a rose-like fragrance. The Shulamite girl speaks of Solomon in Song of Solomon 1:14, "My beloved is to me a cluster of henna blossoms." This is symbolic of how we cherish our beloved, the Lord Jesus Christ. The henna plant is also functional as the leaves are used for hair dye.

3. **Spikenard** is an aromatic oil extracted from an herb, the nard plant. A highly prized perfume comes from the root of this plant. It was very costly because it came from a very remote source. It is native to the mountains of Nepal and Tibet. A long and difficult journey brought

this plant from the east. It was often stored in alabaster boxes that had to be broken to obtain the perfume. It is the perfume of the alabaster box in Mark 14:3 and John 12:3 that Mary of Bethany broke open and poured over Jesus to anoint Him for burial. The Scripture says that the house was filled with the fragrance of the perfume.

Sometimes our walk with the Lord seems remote and lonely, long and difficult, but as we are broken before the Lord, our fragrance is released unto Him from the depths of our being. An acquaintance of mine had a dream of returning to her homeland of Australia with her family to plant a church there. This had been in her heart for many years as the Lord led her family from place to place to serve Him as He directed. There had already been a lot of letting go in her journey, but one day the Lord asked her to let go of her passport. This was very difficult because she was giving up her dream. As she shared with me about this, I saw such a clear picture of how precious this was to the Lord, and I saw the beauty in it and the fragrance that was released through her brokenness.

4. **Saffron** is a product of the crocus flower, made from the stigmas which are dried and pressed into small cakes. It has a variety of practical uses such as flavoring, perfume, and coloring. It was also used medically and speaks of the different ways God uses us, both in practical ways and for the healing of others. Saffron symbolizes the fragrance released in our lives as a result of being "in Him."

5. **Calamus** is a reed, or sweet-smelling cane, known as Indian grass oil. It was part of a mixture used to make the holy anointing oil in Exodus 30:23, and was also used in connection with sacrifice. The bruised leaves of this plant

gave off a fresh, gingery smell that was very much desired and valued in the East. Hebrews 12:1 admonishes us to "present our bodies a living and holy sacrifice, acceptable to God, which is our spiritual service of worship." If we are going to be truly anointed by the Holy Spirit, there will be sacrifice. There will be a *bruising* of our flesh. Christ is our example as He sacrificed Himself for us and He was bruised for our iniquities (Isa. 53:5). When we are bruised, He supports us. "A bruised reed He will not break" (Matt. 12:20, NIV). A reed in the Scriptures is a symbol of weakness. It can be easily broken, and Jesus wants us to know that He is there is with us when we are bruised. He lifts us up, strengthens our weak hands and hearts, and bears us up with His grace, power, tenderness and love.

6. **Cinnamon** was a costly import in biblical times, used as a spice for cooking and perfume, just as it is today. Its usefulness and value comes from the *inner bark* of the cinnamon tree, just as ours comes from our *inner life* with God. It is the *"hidden person* of the heart with the imperishable quality of a gentle and quiet spirit, which is precious in the sight of God" (1 Pet. 3:4, emphasis mine). And as the Apostle Paul prays, "that He would grant you, according to the riches of His glory, to be strengthened with power through His Spirit in the *inner man*" (Eph. 3:16, emphasis mine).

7. **Frankincense** is a gum resin that comes from peeling back layers of bark from a tree until sap exudes in "tears." It has a fragrant balsamic odor and was used as holy incense in Jewish worship. It was placed on the meal offering of first fruits in Leviticus 2:15-16 and on the show bread in Leviticus 24:7. It was significant as a gift from the Magi to the infant Jesus because of its place

in the Jewish worship ceremony. Giving frankincense was an act of worship on their part. Our worship of Christ is a "gift" to Him, and the garden of our heart is the place of worship. Often the sweetest worship of our Lord comes out of the painful experiences of our lives. It happens when He allows our "layers" to be peeled back until we become exposed and vulnerable before Him, "exuding tears."

8. **Myrrh** is an exotic gum resin, and the word means "bitter" in Greek. Its chief use in biblical times was in the holy anointing oil (Ex. 30:23). It was used as a perfume (which was very costly) and also medically to deaden pain. In Mark 15:23, myrrh was mixed with wine and aloes and offered to Jesus when He was on the cross. It was also used in burial preparations of royalty. In John 19:39, Nicodemus brought myrrh and aloes to prepare Christ's body for burial. It seems there is a connection between the anointing of the Holy Spirit, being crucified with Christ in a death to ourselves, and the "bitter" experiences in our lives that often may be required to truly experience that anointing. "You love righteousness and hate wickedness; therefore God, Your God, has set you above your companions by anointing You [reference to Christ] with the oil of joy . . . All Your robes are fragrant with myrrh and aloes and cassia" (Ps. 45:7-8, NIV).

9. **Aloe** is referenced in the Old Testament are as the "aloe tree," a great towering tree 100-200 feet high, which is said to have been planted by the Lord in the garden of Eden (Num. 24:6). The inner wood and resin are fragrant and used in perfumery, and they represent prosperity. It is called "paradise wood" because of a legend saying that Adam brought a shoot of it out of Eden.

The New Testament references to an aloe plant (unique in Scripture and no longer known from nature), speak of the value that came from the leaves. Its bitter juice, a bright violet liquid, was cleansing and healing, and the fibers in the leaves were useful for making cords and nets. The violet liquid was mixed with myrrh and used to embalm Christ's body. The color violet/purple has always been connected with royalty.

Aloe symbolically speaks to us of the benefits of the blood of Christ: cleansing from sin, healing, and the royal position we have in Him. First Peter 2:9 says, "But you are a chosen race, a *royal* priesthood, a holy nation, a people for God's own possession, so that you may proclaim the excellencies of Him who has called you out of the darkness into His marvelous light" (emphasis mine).

When God is in our lives fully and we live in Him fully, He produces a variety of "plants" to spring up in the garden of our heart. We also see that the He allows "winds" to blow across our garden. It is through these experiences that we manifest His grace and become even more fruitful and useful for His glory.

Awake, O north wind, and come, wind of the south,
Make my garden breathe out fragrance, let its spices be wafted abroad.
May my beloved come into *His garden*, and eat its choicest fruits!
—Song of Sol. 4:16, emphasis mine

If it is our desire to be our best for the Lord, then we must allow the cold winds of adversity to blow upon us as well as the temperate, warm south winds. The best apples are grown in northern climates because the frost brings out their choicest, utmost flavor. If you have ever tasted an apple grown in a warm climate, you know they are tasteless and dull. We, too, need times of trial and suffering to bring out the best fruit in us. God is interested in our response to Him during those times, even when we do not understand. Will we continue to trust Him and truly believe in His goodness? Are we willing to allow Him to work out His best for us? These are the times we "breathe out fragrance." These are the times of greatest spiritual growth. Of course, we also need the warmth of the south winds so that we experience great victories. He alone knows the balance necessary for each individual life. His love, grace, goodness, faithfulness, gentleness, and mercy are unchanging, both in times of adversity and in times of victory.

Solomon's garden is a picture of our life in the fullness of the Holy Spirit. It is a result of walking in the garden with the Lord, of being so filled with Him that not only are our hearts refreshed, but living water flows out from us to bless and refresh the world around us. "You are a garden spring, a well of fresh water, and streams flowing from Lebanon" (Song of Sol. 4:15). Here is a well that is full and fresh and life-giving. The Lord wants to give us this as we respond by opening ourselves up to Him and allowing Him to come fully into our heart, trusting Him in every circumstance. It is a relationship of "love within the wall" as we respond to His precious love for us and come into that protected place with Him—the garden that belongs to the Lord.

I have come into my garden, my sister, my bride.
—Song of Sol. 5:1

Chapter 3

REFLECTIONS IN THE GARDEN ...

1. Close your eyes and picture yourself as a fountain, a well of living water, and a flowing stream. How can you experience each of these in your life, and how are they connected?

_____

_____

_____

_____

2. Think about and/or ask the Lord to show you any areas in your life that are not pure (attitudes, words, habits, actions). Ask Him to pour His living water into those areas to bring cleansing and freedom to live the way He wants you to live, pure and free.

_____

_____

_____

_____

3. Reflecting on the plants and trees in Solomon's garden, can you remember a time in your own life when pain and suffering resulted in something beautiful and good and lasting?

_____

_____

_____

_____

4. To which of the plants or trees in Solomon's garden do you most closely relate, and why?

_____

_____

_____

_____

PRAYER

Father God,

Thank you for the beautiful flowers, plants, and trees in Solomon's garden that are so rich in the symbolism of Your love relationship with us. I desire the fullness of all that is found in this garden—for Your best to be worked out in my life, even the times of adversity. Draw me into a place of complete trust in You and cause me to grow spiritually to bear beautiful fruit for Your glory. In Jesus name, amen.

CHAPTER 4

WEEDS IN THE GARDEN

THE WILDERNESS

*Behold, it was completely overgrown with thistles, its surface was
covered with nettles, and its stone wall was broken down.*
—Prov. 24:31

OUR CHALLENGE IS to maintain "love within the wall,"
protecting our intimacy with the Lord and keeping our lives free
of "weeds." The growth of undesirable plants in a garden (weeds,

thorns, and thistles) are often the result of neglect. This is also true with the garden of our heart in our relationship with God. If we do not tend and nurture the garden, the healthy plants will have no room to grow. Proverbs 15:19 says, "The way of the sluggard is overgrown with thorns [it pricks, lacerates, and entangles him], but the way of the righteous is plain and raised like a highway" (TAB). A sluggard is a habitually lazy person, and when we get lax in our relationship with God, our path becomes overgrown and unclear. Thorns are used figuratively in the Bible as "opposition in the path that will obstruct our way."

Just as in a natural garden, we need to be on constant guard against weeds. *You don't have to work at growing weeds*, they just naturally reproduce themselves. One or two may seem like nothing, but the next thing you know, they have multiplied many times over again unless you bring them under control by removing them or applying weed killer.

SIN

What is the origin of weeds and thorns in the garden of the Lord? Genesis 3:18 makes it clear that sin brought about judgment from God, which resulted in the protective wall of the "garden of delight" being broken down and then weeds were introduced: "Cursed is the ground because of you; in toil you shall eat of it all the days of your life. Both thorns and thistles it shall grow for you."

Sin fits the description of a thorn perfectly. It hurts us, blocks our way to God, entangles us, and easily grows and multiplies when left unchecked. A thorn is *leafless,* just as sin is *fruitless.* The purpose of a thorn is to inflict pain and cause hardship. This is what sin does in our lives.

Isaiah makes a reference to the gardens connected with idolatrous and adulterous heathen worship in Isaiah 1:29b-30:

"And you will be embarrassed at the *gardens which you have chosen*. For you will be like an oak whose leaf fades away, or as a garden that has no water" (emphasis mine). Is this not true of us when we choose to worship other gods, turning to sin to try to fill the emptiness in our hearts? When we crowd Jesus out by choosing other things, people, or goals, the garden becomes dry and empty. A vacuum is created in our hearts that only God can fill, and the more we try to fill it with other things, the emptier we become.

Anything that absorbs so much of our attention that we neglect our "first love" becomes a form of idol worship. In the *Bethany Commentary on the New Testament*, Adam Clarke writes, "the seed of the Kingdom can never produce much fruit in any heart until the thorns and thistles of vicious affections and impure desires be plucked up by the roots and burned."[11]

The things we choose to do when we neglect God and turn to the world are different for each one of us. The Bible says in 1 John 2:16 that all that is in the world falls into three categories: the pride of life, lust of the eyes, and lust of the flesh. It may be an immoral relationship, some form of addiction, greed, or selfishness, or it may be just slow seduction into the world's ways, away from the protective wall of the Lord. Whatever it is, it drains the life of God from us. We stop bearing fruit and we become dry, parched ground. A garden that is hard, dry, and cracked is laden with weeds. Lack of water does not prohibit the growth of weeds, but rather seems to encourage them. Lack of the "water" the Word of God provides a lack of the freshness of the Holy Spirit in our lives and blocks our spiritual growth. This lack of the Holy Spirit encourages the growth of sin in our lives. Sin multiplies and soon becomes a very big job to untangle. Our character is to be free of fleshly and sinful pursuits so that God can develop His plan in our lives.

THE ENEMY

Satan was the origin of sin, and he continues his evil work of sowing weeds and tares into the garden of the Lord. The parable of the wheat and the tares in Matthew 13 describes the good seed that Christ sows in the field and the way in which the devil sows tares among the good plants.

Tares are a destructive weed, which in their early stage of growth are almost indistinguishable from wheat. Satan will do everything he can to discredit the work of God in our lives by scattering seeds of evil and allowing doubt to take residence in the soil of our hearts. It is a grievous thing to see tares in the garden of the Lord, where good seed becomes choked out and soil is wasted. God did not intend for this mixture. The Matthew 13 parable represents the hypocritical and the ungodly—those who will be allowed to grow together with the righteous until harvest time, when they will be gathered and burned. We do not want to be counted among the wicked, but rather with the righteous who will "shine forth as the sun in the kingdom of their Father" (Matt. 13:43).

When the enemy plants seeds to oppose God's work, those seeds can grow, become deeply imbedded within us, and attach themselves to us, creating a very unhealthy "root system." The roots of weeds are quickly established and often it is not enough to simply pull out the weeds. As an example in the natural realm, dandelions literally take over beautiful, grassy lawns in the summer months, and it is not adequate to simply pull them out. Strong weed killers must be applied because of the scattering of seeds and the deep root systems. I often see gardeners who are hand-pulling dandelions from their lawns; however, they soon discover (much to their dismay) that they grow back twice as many. The problem with pulling the root is that if the root is not cut off deep enough under the soil, two shoots will grow to replace the one.

Dandelions look so attractive from afar—like a beautiful yellow carpet—yet viewed up close, they have ugly jagged leaves and cause destruction. Sin often looks attractive, but it is a completely destructive force. The problem of sin comes from within—from the root, from the heart. "For from within, out of the heart of men, proceed the evil thoughts, fornications, thefts, murders, adulteries, deeds of coveting and wickedness, as well as deceit, sensuality, envy, slander, pride and foolishness. All these evil things proceed from within and defile the man" (Mark 7:21-23).

We often think the problem comes from external circumstances, but our fight is really within ourselves. We may be faced with circumstances over which we have no control, but the Lord is interested in how we respond to those circumstances. He sees the motivation of our hearts. The enemy will find the weak spot in us and he will devise a scheme against us to bring that weakness out. It can be very subtle at first because that's how he operates—to deceive us and hook us into his ways rather than allowing us to follow God's ways.

I remember a time when someone handed me a bouquet of dandelions. At first, I thought it was such a sweet gesture. Looking back, I realize it was a graphic illustration of the kind of relationship that was being offered. It looked attractive from the outside, but when I looked a little closer, I discovered that the interest of the person was an immoral, deceitful relationship. He was trying to "hook" me into entering into something very destructive. The enemy was subtle in this, making this person look gentle, kind, and giving. There was a longing in me to belong to someone and to be loved. What the enemy did was step into this area of vulnerability, offering a counterfeit of what God wanted for me, thereby opposing God's very plan for my life. The Lord used this to teach me, strengthen me, and show me He had a much better plan.

When we give in, the roots of sin hook deeply into us, and it is very difficult to remove the entanglements. In 2 Peter 2:21, Peter writes, "By what a man is overcome, by this he is enslaved." He goes on to talk about people who have come to know the truth, yet again become entangled and overcome by former sins and how much harder it is to be free of them. If we embrace what we know to be evil, then we are actually taking the "hook" that leads us down a path not intended for us.

ROOTS FROM THE PAST

The weeds in the garden are not just from a sinful lifestyle. They are also things in our heart that are deeply rooted in the past: hurt, rejection, abuse, anger, bitterness, hatred, envy, grief, fear. It is whatever prevents the garden springs from flowing up and out of our lives. These negative emotions actually stop up the well of "living waters." Often, we walk in private pain and have no idea that we need to get free of these debilitating, negative roots. It is very important to spend time with the Lord, asking Him to reveal all of the areas in our lives from which we need to be freed. They are frequently completely unrecognized by us. This is where the Body of Christ comes in to help us. There are many wonderful ministries and people specifically called to help us get free so that we can live in the "whole and complete" manner that God designed for us. Jesus came to set us free from the past. One of the words for salvation, *sozo* in Greek, actually means "to save, make whole, deliver, heal, and preserve."[12]

THE WILDERNESS

There will be times in the life of every believer where we will be led into the "wilderness" just as Jesus was. A wilderness is generally a barren wasteland, dry and uninhabited. The Hebrew word for wilderness describes it as a "pathless waste of the wilderness of wandering." It does not sound like an attractive place to spend any time, yet the isolation of the wilderness is ideal for God's purposes in our lives—teaching us dependence on Him and molding us into His character and likeness. The only problem is that we do not always respond to the wilderness in the way Jesus did, perfectly passing the tests given Him. This means we have to stay there until we "get" what the Lord is trying to do in our lives. In my case, I stayed there a very long time. You see, we have *choices in* the wilderness. We can choose to turn to the Lord and be completely dependent on Him, or we can choose our own way to make it through the wilderness.

Regardless of our circumstances, we are responsible for our behavior. We often want to blame something or someone else, or even God, for our weaknesses and failures. We have a way of rationalizing our choices.

It is interesting to me that frequently the wilderness experience follows a "high" in the walk of a believer. Jesus Himself had just been baptized by the Holy Spirit and then was driven into the wilderness. The Israelites were led through the parting of the Red Sea right into the Wilderness of Sin. Exodus 16:1-2 says, "They set out from Elim and all the congregation of the sons of Israel came to the Wilderness of Sin, which is between Elim and Sinai." Elim was an oasis where there were twelve springs of water and seventy date palms. Elim provided abundant water, provision, and rest. Even though the Lord had just provided abundantly for them, as soon as they came to the wilderness, the Israelites were fearful and complained they would all starve to death. They tested the Lord and wondered whether the Lord was among them. They sinned in the wilderness over and over again, and as a result, they wandered for 40 years, circling the same mountain.

We, too, wonder where God is when we are in the wilderness. Instead of trusting Him, we complain and feel sorry for ourselves and then try to fill the emptiness we feel with other things. The wilderness can either be a time of transformation for us or it can be a wilderness of "sin." When I left the missions experience, I was led into a wilderness. I started out singing, "my life is in you, Lord …" but that pronouncement was severely tested! Through many distressing circumstances, I found myself on a downward spiral. The enemy laid traps for me, and I fell right into them because of my own vulnerability. I failed many of the tests the Lord put before me, so I circled the mountain many times and put more distance between the Lord and me before I understood that He was teaching me to have complete dependence on Him, no matter how abandoned and lost I felt.

I found it much more difficult to break the patterns of sin than to establish them. I fell often, but the Lord was there to pick me up and put me back on track. After really finding victory in a particular area, I failed again miscrably, and felt I would never truly conquer the weaknesses I had. He led me to read more about the Wilderness of Sin in Exodus 17:1. It says, "The sons of Israel *journeyed by stages* from the Wilderness of Sin." The Lord was revealing to me in a very personal way that the way out of this wilderness was going to be in stages. The journey into sin was not immediate and the journey out would not be immediate either. It was a process of obedience and renewal. There are times when it will be immediate and times when it is a longer process.

WEED CONTROL

So how do we control the weeds of sin in our lives? We are all susceptible to temptation. Christ died because of the "weeds" in our lives. He understands our nature, knowing we cannot overcome sin by ourselves.

We have hope to overcome sin because God's Word gives us hope. "In the world you have tribulation, but take courage; I have overcome the world" (John 16:33); "You have overcome the evil one" (1 John 2:13); and "Do not be overcome by evil, but overcome evil with good" (Rom. 12:21).

There is also comfort from His Word: "The Lord knows how to rescue the godly from temptation" (2 Pet. 2:9). He *knows,* even when we do not!

There are certain principles to follow for proper weed control in a garden. Regular care is necessary, care such as feeding on schedule, watering to promote healthy growth, and choking out weeds. Mulch is used for the prevention of weeds, but the material chosen must be pure, free of weed seeds. If weeds do spring up in a garden, they must be pulled or dug out in the early stages when they are small, using care to get all the stems and roots.

We can make spiritual applications from this: feeding ourselves with the Word of God, nurturing our relationship with God, and making a determined effort to turn away from sin.

In leading us out of the weeds of sin, the Lord will always set a choice before us because He has given us free will. He does not want us to follow Him out of obligation or merely because we have to, but because we *want to,* out of our own free will. Our responsibility is to make the choice. Deuteronomy 30:1-3 puts it so beautifully: "So it shall be when all of these things have come upon you, the blessing and the curse, which I have set before you, and you call them to mind … and you return to the Lord your God and obey Him with all your heart and soul according to all that I command you today … then the Lord your God will restore you from captivity, and have compassion on you, and will gather you again from all the peoples where the Lord your God has scattered you."

You see, when we do our part by making the choice to return to Him, God does His part. We have to trust what is on the other side of that step of obedience: His blessings, His strength, restoration, and new LIFE.

He tells us in Deuteronomy 30:11 that obedience to Him *is not too difficult,* nor is it out of reach. It feels so hard when we are hooked on sin. Take the first step, and He will be there to give strength for the second and third steps. Even if they are baby steps, keep taking them until you learn to walk on a straight path without falling. Verses 19-20 say, "So *choose life* in order that you may live ... by loving the Lord your God, by obeying His voice, and by holding fast to Him; *for this is your life* and the length of your days" (emphasis mine).

You see, only the Lord can fulfill your life. The weeds will never satisfy an empty heart. They will never fill us; they will only cause more barrenness. Until Jesus Christ takes first place in our hearts, we will feel empty. Jesus Christ came for people like us sinners, the disobedient, those who have wandered away and who are trying to fill the emptiness in their lives.

Jesus offers us a much better way. He offers the gift of being filled with His Living Water—to actually be filled with *Him.* It is a gift of God; a gift of grace. It is the gift of a Person, the only One who can give us abundant life so that we will be full, not hungry; satisfied, not thirsty. He came to make us whole and complete in Him.

I walked through my garden one summer evening and noticed that one of my bushes and several plants had withered leaves that were yellowed and had holes in them. Taking a closer look, I discovered slugs were attacking and had eaten away at my plants, slowly killing them. That same night, I had a time of reflection and took a closer look at my own heart and saw how I, too, had been attacked from the outside and how "something" had been eating away at my soul. I was reminded how locusts devoured the gardens and vineyards in the books of Joel and Amos because the people did not return to the Lord.

The weeds of sin, the past, and the wilderness do not have to consume us or overcome us. We can overcome because we have the promises and the power of God within us. "Greater is

He who is within you than he that is in the world" (1 John 4:4). Even if we are condemned in our own hearts, "in whatever our heart condemns us, God is greater than our heart" (1 John 3:20).

If you are "in the weeds" in your life, I encourage you to return to the Lord. He has so many promises and so many resources available to bring us out of the weeds. When we return to the Lord, He has a wonderful promise for us in Joel 2:25-26: "Then I will make up to you for the years that the swarming locust has eaten ... and you shall have plenty to eat and be satisfied, and praise the name of the Lord your God, Who has dealt wondrously with you."

The Lord is patient in His dealings with us. He wants us to repent and be restored, and He is there to help us overcome when we turn to Him. We are not alone in this. The Bible is filled with passages where it is very clear that the Lord will help us. One that speaks powerfully to me is out of Isaiah 41:10-14 where these phrases are so encouraging:

"I am with you ... I am your God ... I will strengthen you ... I will help you" (v. 10).

"I will uphold you" (v. 10).

"I am the Lord your God ... I will help you" (v. 13).

"I will help you" (v. 14).

The Lord's heart is for us to return to Him, no matter what we have done or what we have allowed to come into our lives that has displeased Him. That is how the weeds are crowded out and the enemies of our soul are destroyed—through returning to the Lord, believing His Word, and experiencing restoration in our relationship with Him. He will help you overcome the weeds in the garden!

As we experience more and more victory over the weeds in our lives, we move even deeper into the garden with the Lord where He entrusts us to make more choices and to give up our will for His will, as we will see in the garden of Gethsemane.

Chapter 4

REFLECTIONS IN THE GARDEN ...

1. Is there a particular weed or thorn in your life that you would like removed? Do you have an example of something that started seemingly harmless but grew into a big blockage?

   _____

   _____

   _____

   _____

2. What kind of pain have you experienced from this?

   _____

   _____

   _____

   _____

3. Have there been seeds of doubt or darkness in your mind as you pursue the things of God that you can now identify as being planted by the enemy?

   _____

   _____

   _____

   _____

4. Have you spent time in the "wilderness"? If so, think about or share what led up to this.

_____

_____

_____

_____

5. What are some ways and/or choices you can make to become free of the weeds or walk out of the wilderness?

_____

_____

_____

_____

PRAYER

Father God,

Thank you that Your way is always best when I am tempted to allow weeds to crop up in my life. Enable me to have discernment to know the difference between what looks good on the outside and what is truly good on the inside. Reveal the truth when the enemy scatters his seeds based in deception and lies. Help me to see and learn the lessons You are teaching me when I walk in the wilderness. In Jesus' name, amen.

CHAPTER 5

THE GARDEN OF GETHSEMANE

LAYING DOWN OUR WILL

*He went forth with His disciples over the ravine
of Kidron where there was a garden.*

—John 18:1

GETHSEMANE IS A place where issues are settled. It is a place that prepares us for the cross. It is a place of spiritual maturity. Jesus often went alone to this garden called Gethsemane to meditate and pray, and also to be with His disciples. The garden of Gethsemane is located in an olive grove just east of Jerusalem above the Brook Kidron on the eastern side of the Mount of Olives. There is something timeless about an olive grove, whose trees, though gnarled and twisted, flourish and are fruitful, signifying "peace and prosperity." The oil produced from olives is symbolic of "joy and gladness." But at what cost does this wonderful sense of wellbeing come?

The very meaning of Gethsemane, "*oil press*," holds much significance. The olives are allowed to ripen (mature) for production and sometimes are hand picked, but usually they are *beaten* off the branches onto the ground prior to the long and intricate process of pressing and clarifying (cleansing to take out the impurities). In Bible times, the oil was pressed out in one of three ways:

1. Treading on the olives with the feet.
2. Using a pestle and mortar to beat it or crush it out.
3. Grinding in a stone press and vat.

An interesting point here is that oil obtained from olives that were *beaten rather than crushed* were of finer quality and burned more brightly in the lamps used in biblical times. Second Corinthians 4:8 says, "We are afflicted in every way, but not crushed; perplexed, but not despairing; persecuted, but not forsaken; struck down, but not destroyed." The Greek work for afflicted, *thlibo*, means "pressed." It refers to sufferings due to the pressure of circumstances or the antagonism of other people. It is almost always connected with those things that come upon a Christian from the outside that press inward.[13]

Jesus was "pressed" in Gethsemane. What can we learn about this garden from what our Savior Himself experienced? What took place here?

It is a place where we are to be alert—to *keep watch* (Mark 14:34). It is a place of prayer, intercession, and spiritual warfare. It is a place of anguish, grief, agony, and struggle, where there is temptation to turn back from the purposes of God. It is a place of laying down our *will* and our rights. It is where difficult choices are made. It represents our inner struggle with God, and it is often a vulnerable time. Jesus experienced loneliness and betrayal in this garden.

A PLACE TO STAY ALERT—TO KEEP WATCH AND PRAY

Why did Jesus tell His disciples to be alert? Because He knew the enemy was coming. First Peter 5:8 says, "Be of sober spirit, be on the alert. Your adversary, the devil, prowls about like a lion, seeking someone to devour." The chief natural enemy of the olive tree is the locust (the locust devours olive trees). In Scripture, locusts symbolize powerful and large enemy (demonic) armies that seek to destroy and consume the fruits of man's labor. The goal is to reduce the garden of the Lord to a wilderness. Joel 1 speaks prophetically about the devastating work of locusts invading Judah in the "day of the Lord." As a result of the invasion, verse 12 ends with, "Indeed, the rejoicing dries up from the sons of men." Gethsemane is a place to pray and resist the enemy. "But resist him, firm in your faith, knowing that the same experiences of suffering are being accomplished by your brethren who are in the world. After you have suffered for a little while, the God of all grace, who called you to His eternal glory in Christ, will Himself perfect, confirm, strengthen and establish you" (1 Pet. 5:9-10).

A PLACE OF GRIEF, AGONY, AND ANGUISH

In Mark 14:34, Jesus said, "My soul is deeply grieved to the point of death" and Luke 22:44 tells us, "And being in agony, He was praying fervently; and His sweat became like drops of blood, falling down upon the ground." It is difficult to comprehend the depth of His agony, yet we, too, know on a purely human level of understanding what it is like to go through agony and suffering. It is normal to experience grief in our life, not something to be denied, as it is a part of the process of letting go of everything.

TEMPTATION TO TURN BACK FROM
THE PROMISES OF GOD

Even Jesus asked the Father, if He was willing, to remove the cup of suffering. How many times do we cry out to the Lord, "It's too hard!" or "I can't go on!"? We are not alone when we walk the way of Gethsemane, even when we feel alone. The Lord is there and is very aware of the inner struggle with Him and our circumstances.

Friends and family may not understand what we are going through, just as the disciples probably did not understand what Jesus was experiencing or they would have stayed awake. At times, friends are not able to pray as diligently as we expect them to, or to keep watch and be alert like we want them to, or to stay with us in our agony. Even though there is comfort in having those who love us near, it can still be a very lonely place because it represents our "inner struggle" with God, and we alone have to ultimately make the choice to go on with Him.

LAYING DOWN OUR WILL AND OUR RIGHTS

This is a place where difficult choices are made. There is always a Gethsemane before the cross. In the garden, we make up our minds. The goal in Gethsemane is "yet not as I will, but as You will" (Matt. 26:39). In the midst of the struggle, Jesus always came back to this statement. We, too, need always to come back to the same words, deciding for the will of the Lord over our own will. The free will God gave each one of us is a powerful force: strong and stubborn, bent on following its own way. God desires for us to *choose* His way, as this is the highest form of love and worship to Him. Psalm 51:17 says that "a broken and contrite heart, O God, thou wilt not despise" (KJV). After our will is broken before the Lord and we choose to follow Him at all costs, He steps in tenderly to assure us He is there. After Jesus made the difficult choice to continue to the cross, Luke 22:43 says, "An angel from heaven appeared to Him, strengthening Him." God strengthens us for what is ahead.

A PLACE OF GOING FORWARD

"Arise, let us be going" (Matt. 26:46). There is no longer any hesitation, for the decision to stay on the path to the cross has been made. Now it is a matter of rising up and meeting the circumstances head on. It is setting your face like flint (see Isa. 50:7) and not turning back!

BETRAYAL IN THE GARDEN

After Jesus spoke the words, "Get up, let us be going" (Matt. 26:46), He also said, "Behold, the one who betrays Me is at hand." John 18:1-2 tells us "He went forth with His disciples over the ravine of the Kidron, where there was a garden, into which He Himself entered, and His disciples. Now Judas also, who was betraying Him, knew the place; for Jesus had often met there with His disciples."

Jesus was betrayed by a familiar person in a familiar place. This garden had often been a place of refuge for Him, a place of security and fellowship. This is what the church is meant to be for us. We share deep, close relationships in the Body of Christ. And, oh, how we hurt when one of these relationships brings us the kiss of betrayal.

There is something significant about the fact that Jesus had to cross over the Brook Kidron on his way to the cross. Each year in Old Testament times, a red cow was led over the Brook Kidron on a specially-constructed bridge (which spanned this deep, rock-ribbed ravine) to the Mount of Olives to be sacrificed for the atonement of the people. Now the Son of God, the innocent Lamb who would take away the sins of the world, followed the same path across the Kidron. It is also the same ravine David had to cross when he was fleeing from one who betrayed him: his own son, Absalom.

The Brook Kidron was actually a dark ravine that was dry most of the year, except during winter storms, when it became a torrent—a violent, rushing stream swollen by the suddenness of the rains. *Kidron* is translated as "dark" and "turbid" and means the depths of degradation and misery, producing obscurity, hidden by darkness, secluded and remote. The Brook Kidron is symbolic of what both David and Jesus experienced there. How degrading was it for David to have his own son turn on him, forcing him to give up his throne and flee? Jesus also experienced an extremely dark time, knowing one of his own had already sold his soul to betray Him. Reverend Alban Goodier, in his book, *The Passion and Death of Christ* writes, "the nearer the betrayer is to our heart, the nearer our own heart is to the heart of Jesus in the garden."[14]

It is interesting that Jesus did not talk to his disciples about those outside of their circle who would cause Him to suffer and crucify Him; rather, He focused his last conversations with them on the betrayal, desertion, and denial of those closest to Him, as these were the things that troubled Jesus in His heart. We can bear what outsiders do to us, but it is very difficult to bear being hurt or betrayed by the ones we love (those in our inner circle, especially family members or brothers and sisters in Christ). Jesus went through the utter loneliness of betrayal by someone close to Him. No one can take the place of another and bear this kind of pain. It is simply a lonely time. However, we do have One who understands and One who will never turn His back on us. He will never leave us or forsake us (see Heb. 13:5). Jesus is our hope, and He is our comfort to bring us across to the "other side" of the Brook Kidron.

A garden of Gethsemane experience for us is an extremely vulnerable time. We are seemingly pressed from all sides. It is a time of agony and desolation, where we can so easily fall to temptations, give up, and take another way. Gethsemane is a place of choices, where our will is broken for His will. We need to follow the pathway of Jesus and walk to Gethsemane, no matter how close to being crushed our souls and spirits feel. It is this "pressing" that produces the oil of joy and gladness and the oil of anointing from the Holy Spirit. Deuteronomy 32:13 says that olive oil is produced out of the "flinty rock," a most unlikely location that suggests something of great value can be produced out of what appears to be an unproductive place. This is what God does in and through us in the garden of Gethsemane. He brings forth the fruit of the olive tree.

Jesus went before His disciples to wrestle with His own will. "Sit here, while I go over there and pray" (Matt. 26:36). "He went a little beyond them and fell to the ground and began to pray" (Mark 14:35). He went further and *deeper* into the interior of the garden. As we follow Jesus on the path of the struggle of the will, our own Gethsemane experiences lead us into the *deeper things of God* and growth in spiritual maturity. This is the garden of Gethsemane.

Chapter 5

REFLECTIONS IN THE GARDEN ...

1. Is there a time when you had to pray through something in a deep way, resisting a strong pull to turn back or to give up? What was the outcome?

   _____

   _____

   _____

   _____

2. Reflect on a lonely time in your life when you felt it was just too hard to go on. How do you think Jesus can relate to this? Has there been a time when you chose to obey the Lord and what He has asked you to do, even when you had no support from others?

   _____

   _____

   _____

   _____

3. Have you ever been betrayed by someone close to you? How did you deal with it?

_____

_____

_____

_____

PRAYER

Father God,

Thank you that the garden of Gethsemane is a place of growing inner strength in You as my own will and the enemy's plans are broken. Help me keep going when the choices are hard. Enable me to be drawn into a deeper place of prayer during these times where I can hear Your voice when I am tempted to give up. In Jesus' name, amen.

CHAPTER 6

THE GARDEN OF CRUCIFIXION

DYING TO SELF

That which you sow does not come to life unless it dies.
—1 Cor. 15:36

THE GARDEN OF my heart seems so empty, so desolate—as if it is late autumn and all the fruit has been picked off the trees, the flowers have withered and died, and the leaves have all fallen, scattered and blown away by the wind. There seems to be nothing left. What has become of me? I find no answers, just a deep sense of emptiness. Where are you, Lord? You haven't moved or changed, Father. Yet I cannot find you anymore. I want so much to be with You, sharing the same love relationship we've had for so long.

I wrote these words in my journal after months of feeling a sense of "the wilderness" in my spiritual life with God. What happened to that wonderful sense of intimacy I shared with God? Where was the "garden enclosed" that is so beautifully depicted in the Song of Solomon? Not only was my inner spirit suffering from God's apparent absence, but there was no visible external fruit being produced in my life. I was experiencing spiritual "barrenness." During a time like this, it may feel as if there is no growth, but this is a necessary season for the garden of our hearts to produce what the Lord purposes for us according to His timing. It is a time to let go of personal hopes and ambitions and "die to self."

Jesus Christ died to self. What happened when He was crucified? What was His response to His own suffering? What can we learn from Jesus and apply to our own times of suffering?

STRIPPING

"They stripped Him … and mocked Him" (Matt. 27:28-29). "Then the soldiers, when they had crucified Jesus, took His outer garments" (John 19:23).

It was the custom for a victim's garments to be taken and divided among executioners. Jesus was not only stripped of His outer garments, but of His very character. Who He was, in the eyes of man, was also stripped away. He was misunderstood, verbally abused, mocked, shamed, and humiliated. The Bible says, "[He] was numbered with transgressors" (Isa. 53:12). In other words, Jesus was counted by man as "evil" and placed in the same league as robbers and murderers. Crucifixion was reserved for the guiltiest criminals, and here Christ took our transgressions and our guilt, when He himself was sinless perfection.

What did it feel like to be fulfilling God's purposes, yet be accused by man of being on the enemy's side? What did it feel like to be that misunderstood?

Jesus was *stripped* inside and out. Jesus calls us to be stripped when He says, "If anyone would come after me, he must deny himself and take up his cross and follow me" (Matt. 16:24, NIV). We are to lay down our own selfish interests (and even our "not so selfish" interests) and endure misunderstanding, shame, and possibly a tarnished reputation, just as He did. The response of Jesus to the stripping process was endurance ... "for the joy set before Him endured the cross, despising the shame" (Heb. 12:2). Jesus saw beyond the shame to the eternal purpose of the Father that was ahead on the cross.

While reading about Christ's journey to the cross during one Holy Week, I was struck by what happened during the beginning of the triumphal entry into Jerusalem. We often focus on the palm branches that the people were waving as He rode in on the colt, but the Lord showed me something new about this in Luke 19:36. This verse says, "As He was going, they were spreading their coats on the road." Even though they were not aware of it, they were preparing the way for the new garments Jesus was soon to provide through His death on the cross and His resurrection. I wept when I read this because it was such a clear picture of us taking off our old, filthy garments (stripping off our old sin natures) and spreading them on the ground under the feet of Jesus. Our sins are "under His feet." It's only when we are stripped of the old garments that we can put on the new garments that Jesus Christ has provided for us.

INTENSE SUFFERING

Jesus went through intense physical suffering even before the actual crucifixion. One condemned to crucifixion was first flogged with a whip with metal tips on the ends of the thongs that would tear up the flesh. After a night of unimaginable torture, his wrists and feet were then nailed to the cross to begin a slow and painful death that was accomplished by intense thirst, exhaustion, and exposure. Jesus Christ endured physical suffering, emotional suffering, and spiritual suffering to which we could not begin to relate; yet the Father had a purpose in this suffering—the redemption of mankind and the ultimate reconciliation to the Father.

There are purposes we do not see in our own suffering, whether physical, emotional, or spiritual, and our response is to be one of "looking beyond" as Jesus did. Once again, we have a choice in this garden of crucifixion. We can choose to focus on ourselves or focus on the Lord. It is a choice of despair and loss of hope, or a choice of trust in the ultimate plans and purposes of God. It is very difficult to respond with trust when we are in the midst of suffering. One of the reasons it is so hard is because of our lack of understanding about why we are suffering. It seems easier to endure suffering when we know the reason for our pain. The answers often come later in our journey with the Lord, or they may never be fully clear to us. In spite of this, He asks us to trust Him. I recall a time when I was going through intense suffering and I asked a friend to pray for me. She shared later that while praying, she saw a picture of a dense forest that I could not see through, over, or around, but on the other side was a beautiful green meadow. The message was that even though I could not "see beyond" my present circumstances, there was life on the other side of it.

Jesus was treated unjustly, and the Word of God speaks very clearly to us about this type of suffering. There are biblical principles we can learn about being treated unjustly.

WE HAVE BEEN CALLED FOR THIS PURPOSE

"But if when you do what is right and suffer for it, and you patiently endure it this finds favor with God. For you have been called for this purpose, since Christ also suffered for you, leaving you an example for you to follow in His steps, who committed no sin, nor was any deceit found in His mouth; and while being reviled, He did not revile in return; while suffering, He uttered no threats, but kept entrusting Himself to Him who judges righteously."

—1 Pet. 2:20-23

There is so much in this passage to absorb into our hearts and act on:

1. We are called to *patiently endure* when we suffer.
2. God's *favor is given to us* when we respond in patient endurance. First Peter 3:14 states, "If you suffer for the sake of righteousness, you are blessed" and 1 Peter 3:17 says, "It is better, if God should will it so, that you suffer for doing what is right rather than for doing what is wrong."
3. We are to *follow the example* of Christ. He did not sin and no deceitful or threatening words came out of His mouth. Jesus did not revile in return, but He trusted the Father to do the judging.

WE LEARN OBEDIENCE

"Although He was a Son, He learned *obedience* from the things which He suffered" (Heb. 5:8). Jesus was never disobedient, yet this verse implies that His obedience did not come from His position in the godhead as Son, but rather from experiencing suffering. Philippians 2:8 tells us that Jesus "humbled Himself by becoming obedient to the point of death, even death on a cross."

Throughout the New Testament we are directed to "take up our cross daily" (Luke 9:23), "share in the sufferings of Christ"

(1 Pet. 4:13), and "suffer hardship with me, as a good soldier of Christ" (2 Tim. 2:3). Suffering seems to be a required part of following Christ, and we cannot expect to be exempt from it. If Jesus learned obedience through suffering, how much more must we learn obedience through the same? Jesus carried out obedience to the will of God by giving His own life. Isaiah 50:7 speaks prophetically of Christ, where it is written, "I have set My face like flint." Flint symbolizes the steadfastness of the Servant of the Lord and in this verse, reveals His total obedience, especially in the sufferings leading to His death. We are also asked to give our lives to God and be obedient and steadfast in whatever God requires of us. The only way we can do this is by relying on the power of the Holy Spirit within us.

THE POWER OF SIN IS BROKEN THROUGH SUFFERING

"Therefore since Christ has suffered in the flesh, arm yourselves with the same purpose, because he who has suffered in the flesh has ceased from sin, so as to live the rest of the time in the flesh no longer for the lusts of men, but for the will of God."

—1 Pet. 4:1-2

Again, Christ is our example and we are admonished to look at suffering from His perspective. Look at how the dominion of sin was broken by the suffering of Jesus on the cross. The principle for us is that there is something about suffering that breaks down sin in our lives. New life is on the other side of suffering! God does not allow suffering to punish us, but to conform us into the image of His dear Son and to bring us into a place of new life in Christ.

The Lord can use us for His purposes while we are suffering. We read story after story of people who have suffered tremendously, but in the midst of it are the ones who give hope, encouragement, and inspiration to others. There was a young mother who lost her hands and feet to amputation due to an infection that ravaged her body after giving birth to her child. All she wanted to do was to get on with life so she could get home to care for her baby. She saw beyond her own suffering. A young boy with terminal muscular dystrophy had big goals in his young life and accomplished them all before dying, leaving a legacy of inspiration to many. A man who was convicted unjustly and spent many years in prison, used this time to start a Bible study and minister to other inmates, bringing many to the Lord instead of turning away from the Lord and embracing bitterness and lack of forgiveness. These are just three of countless stories told of perseverance even when life deals some serious blows. There can be growth, beauty, fruit, and new life in the midst of suffering in the garden of Crucifixion.

Father James Groenings, in his book, *History of the Passion*, writes about how our precious Lord arrived at the "Garden Gate," named for the beautiful garden which lay just outside of Calvary and stretched around the foot of it. Calvary was the hill that was about to bear the *Tree of Life*, our Redeemer.[15] When sin entered the world in the garden of Eden, man no longer had access to the Tree of Life. In the crucifixion, Jesus restored our access to the Tree of Life and provided a way for us by His death and resurrection. He became the Tree of Life for us, giving us new life and nourishment in every way. He branched out into every area of our lives. This is the path to the restoration of the Garden of the Lord.

In the place where He was crucified, there was a garden.
—John 19:41

Chapter 6

REFLECTIONS IN THE GARDEN ...

1. Think about times you have endured suffering. Are there any lessons you learned through suffering? Can you identify purpose(s) in a time of trial/suffering?

_____

_____

_____

_____

2. Do you have an example of learning obedience through suffering?

_____

_____

_____

_____

3. How can we respond to suffering and trials in a way that would be pleasing to the Lord?

_____

_____

_____

_____

4. What are the "new garments" Christ provided for us?

_____

_____

_____

_____

PRAYER

Father God,

Thank you for sending Your Son as a sacrifice for our sins. Thank you, Lord Jesus, for laying down Your life for us. You endured the cross to give us forgiveness of our sins and eternal life with You that begins the moment we believe and open our hearts to You. Teach me to respond in the right way during times of trial and suffering and to learn obedience and a deeper trust in Your purposes for my life. In Jesus' name, amen.

.

CHAPTER 7

RESTORATION OF THE GARDEN OF THE LORD

THE ABUNDANT LIFE

He will comfort all her waste places. And her wilderness He will make like Eden, And her desert like the garden of the Lord.
—Isaiah 51:3

BECAUSE OF THE Lord's love and compassion for His people, His desire has always been to restore our lives to be like the garden of Eden—the Garden of the Lord. This restoration was accomplished through Jesus Christ. When man sinned, the

THE GARDEN OF THE LORD

door to the garden existence was shut; but then through the death and resurrection of Christ the door was opened to us. It was through the second Adam (Jesus Christ) that this was made possible. We, through sin, walked out of the garden and closed the door on God. Through Christ, God bids us to come back into the garden where He is, where we can enjoy Him and find delight in Him.

The word "restore" means "to bring back to or put back into a former or original state; to put or bring back into existence or use; to renew." These definitions from the Merriam-Webster *online* dictionary are *in line* with God's plan for us.

God's heart is to give us abundant life, so clearly described in John 10:10. "The thief comes only to steal and kill and destroy; I came that they may have life, and have it abundantly." His promise goes even beyond that in Ephesians 3:20. "Now to Him who is able to do exceedingly abundantly beyond all that we could ask or think, according to the power that works within us."

He wants to fill the empty places in our lives with His love and comfort. He wants to take our wilderness places and make them like Eden. He wants to change our barren, desert places into the beauty and abundance of the garden of the Lord. *He wants to restore us!*

There is no set formula for restoration. It begins with a conscious choice to turn away from our own ways, and it begins with a genuine heart to follow God. Restoration is a journey, not a feeling. It is a *day by day* journey, often taken using small steps. When an antique piece of furniture is restored to its original condition, it takes time. First there is the evaluation of what needs to be done, how extensive the repairs will be, and what tools and materials are necessary. Then there is the stripping away of what is often old—peeling varnish and paint—a messy, but necessary step in order to reveal the grain of the original raw wood. There might be damage to the original surface which needs to be filled in or repaired. Then it is ready for new stain or paint and layers of a fine varnish to restore the piece to its original luster.

When we make the choice to trust, honor, and obey the Lord in the daily out-working of our lives, He *knows* what we need to make our way back to Him. He knows how much of the "old" has to come off; He knows what tools are necessary; He knows the raw material He has to work with. He knows how to restore us. I love thinking about the layers with which he wants to overlay us to bring out the original "luster" that He designed so that we can shine.

In my personal experience, there had been a gradual loss of hope in my life that I wasn't even aware of. It began with a loss of vision and purpose. The Bible says that "where there is no vision, the people perish" (Prov. 29:18, KJV). I felt like I was dying inside. I did not feel that I had any purpose in life. Instead of waiting on God and standing in faith, I gave up and spiraled into depression. This process was slow and subtle, a gradual wearing down spiritually until I no longer had the desire to "fight the good fight keeping faith and a good conscience" (1 Tim. 1:18).

When I first attempted to get myself out of the wilderness, I pursued hope. I had experienced a loss of hope, so I thought if I could only recapture hope, I would be restored. Pursuing hope in itself does not work. During a time of intense discouragement, the Lord showed me two things: instead of pursuing hope, pursue Jesus Christ, the giver of hope. This is the most important thing we can do. Even when there is no one or nothing else to cling to and we have lost all hope, Jesus Christ is there. When we cling to Him, we will come out on the other side of the wilderness and the darkness of what we are going through in life. We will come into His light. The other thing the Lord showed me was that I should change my "earthly" definition of hope. I was looking for life here on earth to stop disappointing me. I was looking to have the empty places in my heart filled through other people. God uses people to help and encourage us, but they are not the answer to hopelessness. When the Bible speaks of hope, it is with an eternal, heavenly perspective. It is a looking forward to all God has in store for us because of all we have been given when Christ gave His life for us. The Lord is the only One who can fill us with true hope.

Jesus had hope beyond the cross. He always kept an eternal perspective, even when He carried the weight of our sin on the cross. "Who for the joy set before Him, endured the cross" (Heb. 12:2).

If we have been living in the weeds of sin, we too carry the weight of it unless we come to Jesus and receive forgiveness and cleansing through His shed blood. If we are living outside of God's ways, we have experienced broken fellowship with Him and separation from Him. It does not mean He is no longer our Father, but we need to be restored to a right relationship with Him. When our children are disobedient and rebellious, we still have the parent-child relationship, but the relationship is out of order and we do not share the same warmth and intimacy we once had. There is so much joy for us when a prodigal child returns, and it gives the Lord joy beyond measure when we return to Him.

There are also times spent in the wilderness that are not connected with a sinful lifestyle. Perhaps it has just become too hard to go on, or there is too much suffering, heartache, disillusionment, and brokenness. This is the time to turn our face from looking down in despair, or around at the overwhelming circumstances, and *look up* to our Lord, who desires to restore us and give us His abundant life.

When I made a conscious decision to lift my face to the Lord and to choose Him above all, He began a restorative work in my life. He came bearing a gift—the gift of hope. Hope in Who He is, hope in His love for me, hope in His purposes for my life, and hope in His personal care for me.

It is only when Jesus Christ lights a candle in the dark corners of our lives that we can have hope. There is a quote by Corita

Kent that says, "Flowers grow out of dark moments." Have you ever noticed how flowers turn their faces towards the sun? They come up out of the dark soil and reach upward to the light and warmth of the sun.

In the beginning, hope may begin as a tiny flicker of flame, so small you hardly recognize it, but as you move nearer to the Lord, the flame becomes brighter, warmer, and larger. That is when we start to experience what intimacy with the Lord is like. If you have never experienced it before, you will be amazed at how life-giving and restorative that relationship is.

There are many examples in the Bible of how Jesus restored people physically that can be applied to spiritual and emotional healing as well. Jesus healed a man with a withered hand (see Mark 3:1-5). He said to the man, "Get up and come forward," and "Stretch out your hand. And he stretched it out, and his hand was restored." The Greek word here for "restore" means to return to the former condition of wholeness. Jesus wants us to get up, face Him, walk towards Him, give Him our hand, and allow Him to restore our lives. He came to make us whole! He is the only one who can do it!

In Mark 8:22-25, a blind man's sight is restored gradually. Jesus first spit on his eyes and laid hands on him and the man could see shapes and forms. "Then again He laid His hands upon his eyes; and he looked intently and was restored, and began to see everything clearly." The lesson we learn from this passage is that restoration may be gradual. It may take time, but when Jesus restores us, our world becomes clear again. The darkness of sin and clouds of confusion and despair are lifted and cleared from our hearts and lives.

Throughout this process of restoration, there is a tremendous need for prayer and time spent in the Word of God. Psalm 119:130 says, "The unfolding of Your words gives light." Praying directly from the Bible is light-giving and life-giving. I love the image of the "unfolding" of God's Word. It is healing to open it, spread it out, remove the coverings from it, and disclose it to view, gradually revealing the written or spoken explanation and making known God's Word. Prayer is healing.

Accountability through fellowship with other mature believers is also extremely important. As I went deeper into the wilderness, I went deeper into isolation, to the point where I didn't want to be with others. I felt it was safer to be by myself. That was deception. I needed to be with believers who could stand with me in prayer and support. Galatians 6:1 says, "Even anyone is caught in a trespass, you who are spiritual, restore such a one in a spirit of gentleness." The Greek word here for "restore" means to mend, furnish completely, and perfectly join together. The tense is continuous present, suggesting the need for patience and perseverance as it occurs. This is a beautiful picture of how the body of Christ is to function. *We need each other!* We must not give up on ourselves or on one another, but rather, we must continue persevering on the road to restoration.

The Lord once gave me a picture when I was praying (see below) to encourage some very dear friends who live totally by faith and dependence on Him. Their hearts were to follow the Lord on the "Highway of Holiness," which is depicted in Isaiah 35 and is a description of the millennial kingdom where we will experience *restoration* in all of its fullness and completeness. These friends were experiencing some very difficult parts of the road in their journey of faith. The Lord showed me that yes, there is rough ground, there are brick walls, there are clouds, roadblocks, and time spent in the wilderness. The enemy will say "go back" or "take a detour" or worse yet, "stop." This is when we are to *persevere and go on with God* in spite of our circumstances. This picture depicts the rough part of the road, but when we persevere and endure, God's purposes are accomplished, and we experience His blessings. We are promised in many passages in the Bible that He will lead us on the right path. Psalm 16:11 says,

"You will make known to me the path of life; in Your presence is fullness of joy, in your right hand there are pleasures forever."

The Highway of Holiness-Path to Restoration

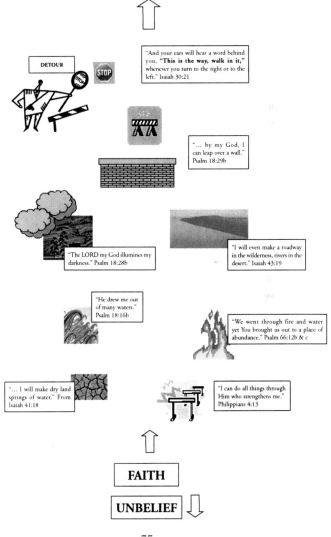

"And your ears will hear a word behind you, **"This is the way, walk in it,"** whenever you turn to the right or to the left." Isaiah 30:21

"... by my God, I can leap over a wall." Psalm 18:29b

"The LORD my God illumines my darkness." Psalm 18:28b

"I will even make a roadway in the wilderness, rivers in the desert." Isaiah 43:19

"He drew me out of many waters." Psalm 18:16b

"We went through fire and water yet You brought us out to a place of abundance." Psalm 66:12b & c

"... I will make dry land springs of water." From Isaiah 41:18

"I can do all things through Him who strengthens me." Philippians 4:13

DETOUR

STOP

FAITH

UNBELIEF

The Lord has a promise for every obstacle we face and we are not alone on this journey. The imprint of the hand of God is upon us, and underneath are His "everlasting arms" (Deut. 33:27). Our God is above, beneath, and before His people as an eternal refuge. The handprint of God cannot be seen in a garden where the soil is hard, dry, and cracked. It is only in soil that is soft and able to be worked that the impression of the hand of God is clearly visible. Our hearts must be kept soft and humble before the Lord so that our lives clearly reflect the character of Jesus Christ as we journey through this life.

One day, as I was in the process of moving nearer to Jesus, He showed me this passage: "Seek the Lord while He may be found; call upon Him while He is near. Let the wicked forsake his way and the evil man his thoughts; and let him return to the Lord, and He will have compassion on him, and to our God, for He will abundantly pardon" (Isa. 55:6-7).

I had once taken the way of thorns and nettles, but as the Lord led me back to Himself, I gave my own ways up to Him. The result of forsaking our own way and turning to Him is that we experience the compassion of the Lord and abundant forgiveness. And there is much more than that! Isaiah 55:12-13 says that we will "go out with joy and be led forth with peace; and instead of the thorn bush, the cypress will come up; and instead of the nettle, the myrtle will come up." The wood from a cypress tree is hard, fragrant, and almost indestructible. It was widely used in ancient times wherever strong, enduring wood was needed. Solomon used it in the building of the temple.

Myrtle is a beautiful flowering shrub, known for its fragrant leaves and was used as a perfume and to adorn banquet rooms for nobility. Is this not a picture of restoration? To experience the joy that comes from intimacy with the Lord, to be strong and find endurance in the Lord, and to bear the fruit of usefulness in the kingdom of God, to be the fragrance of Christ to God and to others that 2 Corinthians 2:15 speaks of?

In a daily devotional calendar, Roy Lessin writes an encouraging thought: "God's purpose is never to destroy us, but always to restore us. The enemy is the destroyer, but God has promised to restore the things the enemy has taken from our lives—all the years of lost joy, all the times of frustration and defeat, all the moments of regret, all the pains of lost opportunities, all the hurts of broken relationships. God is building His kingdom within you—a kingdom of joy, love, peace, righteousness, victory, redemption, and right relationships."[16]

God's heart is for restoration to that place of sweet fellowship and intimacy with Him that will be reflected in every part of our lives. He wants to draw us out, away from self and the destruction we and/or the enemy bring. He has a tender, loving heart for His people. He says, "Arise, my darling, my beautiful one, and come along. For behold, the winter is past, the rain is over and gone. The flowers have already appeared in the land." (Song of Sol. 2:10-12). It is as if He is saying, "The harshness of the wilderness is gone now. Come, walk with me once again in the garden." Our God is inviting us to share in the delights of His company and love. This is the restoration of the Garden of the Lord.

There was a time when I decided to give up on writing this book. I was at a place where it seemed there was more despair in my life than anything else. How could I possibly write about the garden of the Lord? It continues to amaze me how the Lord brings the exact encouragement we need to give us the strength and the vision to go on to accomplish His purposes. The day after I told God that I could not write the book, I received a single sheet of paper from a dear Jamaican girl I had developed a friendship with while we were doing missionary work in Jamaica. This girl lived high on a hill above the village where there was no electricity or running water, and all of their cooking was done over an open fire. She lived in abject poverty in a small hut with several others. She was not, however, poor in spirit.

She had handwritten in broken English these words from a beautiful old hymn and she mailed it to me at exactly the time that I needed it (The following words are written exactly as I received them from her).

this is A Song

Come to the garden alone while the dew is still and the rose; And the voice I hear falling on my ear, the Son of God discloses.

And He walks with me and He talks with me and He tells me I am His own and the joy we share as we tarry there, none other has ever known.

He speaks and the sound of His voice is so sweet, the birds hush their singing and the melody that He gave to me within my heart is ringing.

I stay in the garden with Him though the night around me is falling,

But He bids me go there, for His voice, His voice to me is calling.

And He walks with me and He talks with me and He tells me I am His own; and the joy we share as we tarry there, none other has ever known.

I cannot describe the emotions I felt when I read her letter. This precious song was the message of the whole book: coming to God, walking with Him, listening to Him, belonging to Him, staying with Him even though darkness is all around, and sharing sweet joy with Him.

John Henry Jowett has said, "The Bible opens with a garden. It closes with a garden. The first is the Paradise that was lost. The last is the Paradise regained. Between the two there is a third, the garden of Gethsemane. And it is through the desolation of Gethsemane that we find again the glorious garden through which flows 'a pure river of the water of life. Eden … Gethsemane … New Jerusalem. The journey has been costly and difficult. Yet through it all, God's purposes triumph. His grace, His goodness, His Gethsemane have all made it possible for you and me to dwell in the garden of God forever—a garden in which there is no curse or darkness, only face-to-face fellowship with the Creator."[17] We can dance with joy, for Jesus Christ has restored us to the "garden of delight." He has restored us to our Father!

I was once asked, "What is it like for you in the garden with the Lord?" For me, it feels very private and protected. It's a really safe place. It's a place where I feel peaceful with Him. I feel loved in His presence. It's a soft, gentle place where I can almost hear His footsteps ... It's a place where I know there is always more that He wants to share with me and give to me. It's a beautiful, refreshing place.

My prayer is that each one of us will respond to His invitation: "Come ... come to the Garden of the Lord."

Chapter 7

REFLECTIONS IN THE GARDEN ...

1. Meditate on John 10:10. What does "abundant life" mean to you?

_____

_____

_____

_____

2. When you need hope, who or what do you turn to?

_____

_____

_____

_____

3. Read a verse from Scripture that has special meaning to you or select a new one. Ask the Lord to "unfold" His light to you as you read it. Share or write down anything He shows you.

_____

_____

_____

_____

4. Reflect on the "Highway of Holiness" illustration. Are there parts of this that you can relate to? Read Isaiah 35 and pick out specific promises that speak to you.

_____

_____

_____

_____

5. What is an area of your life that you would like restored? Ask the Lord to restore you.

_____

_____

_____

_____

PRAYER

Father God,

Thank you for Your heart of love for us and that You long for us to look to You for restoration in our lives. Thank you for providing the way for us to be restored to You and dwell forever in the Garden of the Lord through Jesus Christ. I give my heart to You completely—as a garden belonging only to You. In Jesus' name, amen.

ENDNOTES

1. W. E. Vine, *An Expository Dictionary of New Testament Words* (Old Tappan, NJ: Fleming H. Revell Co, 1966), 207.

2. Committee of Scholars and Editors, *Wycliffe Bible Encyclopedia* (Chicago: Moody Press, 1975), 1360.

3. *Webster's Ninth New Collegiate Dictionary* (Springfield: Merriam-Webster Inc., 1985), 506.

4. Roy Lessin, *Never Forgotten ... Always Loved!: Affirming the Heart and Mind of God Toward You* (Siloam Springs, AK: Day Spring Cards, 1992).

5. Wikipedia: www:wikipedia.com.

6. Frances J. Roberts, *Come Away My Beloved* (Ojai: King's Farspan, Inc., 1973), 105, 146.

7. James H. Strong, *Strong's Exhaustive Concordance* (Grand Rapids, MI: Baker Book House, 1987), 42.

8. Charles Caldwell Ryrie, Th.D., *The Ryrie Study Bible* (Chicago: Moody Press, 1978), 1337.

9. ©1986 by Integrity's Hosanna! Music, all rights reserved.

10. H. A. Ironside, *Addresses on the Song of Solomon* (New Jersey, Loizeaux Brothers, Inc., 1973), 77.

11. Adam Clark, *The Bethany Commentary on the New Testament* (Minneapolis, MN: Bethany House Publishers, 1983), 114.

12. James H. Strong, *Greek Dictionary of the New Testament* (Grand Rapids, MI: Moody Press, 1947), 70.

13. W.E. Vine, *An Expository Dictionary of New Testament Words* (Old Tappan, NJ: Fleming H. Revell Co, 1966), 38.

14. Rev. Aglan Goodier, *The Passion and Death of Christ* (New York: P. J. Kennedy & Sons), 166.

15. Rev. James Groenings, *The History of the Passion* (South Bend: Marian Publications, 1975), 251.

16. Roy Lessin, *Never Forgotten ... Always Loved!: Affirming the Heart and Mind of God Toward You* (Siloam Springs, AK: Day Spring Cards, 1992), March 9.

17. John Henry Jowett, *My Daily Meditation for the Circling Year,* "The Three Gardens," February 22. www.preceptaustin.org.

BIBLIOGRAPHY

The Amplified Bible. Grand Rapids: Zondervan Publishing House, 1986.

Ryrie, Charles Caldwell, Th.D. *The Ryrie Study Bible* (NAS). Chicago: Moody Press, 1978.

Vine, W.E. *An Expository Dictionary of New Testament Words.* Old Tappan: Fleming H. Revell Company, 1066.

Committee of Scholars and Editors. *Wycliffe Bible Encyclopedia.* Chicago: Moody Press, 1975.

Strong, James H. *Strong's Exhaustive Concordance.* Grand Rapids: Baker Book House, 1987.

Krumacher, F.W. *The Suffering Savior—Meditations on the Last Days of Christ.* Chicago: Moody Press, 1947.

Groenings, The Reverend James. *The History of the Passion.* South Bend: Marion Publications, 1975.

Habich, John. *"Planting a Garden of Memories,"* Minneapolis: Star Tribune Newspaper, November 12, 1994.

Webster's Ninth New Collegiate Dictionary. Springfield: Merriam-Webster Inc., Publishers, 1985.

Goodier, Reverend Aglan. *The Passion and Death of Christ.* New York: P. J. Kennedy & Sons, 1958.

Nee, Watchman. *The Song of Songs.* Anaheim: Living Stream Ministry, 1993.

Ironside, H. A. *Addresses on the Song of Solomon.* New Jersey: Loizeaux Brothers, Inc., 1973.

Heckel, Dr. Helmar. *"The Heartbeat of Servanthood."* Navarre: Bay Wind Church, November 11, 1998 (used with permission).

Roberts, Frances J. *Come Away My Beloved.* Ojai: King's Farspan, Inc., 1973.

Henry, Matthew. *The Bethany Parallel Commentary on the New Testament and others.* Minneapolis: Bethany House Publishers, 1983.

WinePressPublishing
Great Books, Defined.

To order additional copies of this book call:
1-877-421-READ (7323)
or please visit our website at
www.WinePressbooks.com

If you enjoyed this quality custom-published book,
drop by our website for more books and information.

www.winepresspublishing.com
"Your partner in custom publishing."

CPSIA information can be obtained at www.ICGtesting.com
Printed in the USA
BVOW041913100213

312827BV00002B/13/P

9 781414 122397